Smoking

JUDITH ANDERSON

W
FRANKLIN WATTS
LONDON•SYDNEY

First published in 2004 by Franklin Watts
338 Euston Road, London NW1 3BH

Franklin Watts Australia, Hachette Children's Books,
Level 17/207 Kent Street, Sydney, NSW 2000

Series editor: Sarah Peutrill
Designed by: Pewter Design Associates
Series design: Peter Scoulding
Illustration: Mike Atkinson and Guy Smith, Mainline Design
Picture researcher: Diana Morris
Series consultant: Wendy Anthony, Health Education Unit, Education Service,
Birmingham City Council
Picture credits:
Jerry Arcieri/Corbis: 8c. Paul Baldesare/Photofusion. Posed by models: front cover.
Baumgartner Olivia/Corbis Sygma: 41cr. Norm Betts/Rex Features: 33bl. Richard
Bickel/Corbis: 8bl. Ed Bock/Corbis: 20b. BSIP, Alexandre/SPL: 23c. BSIP, Laurent/SPL: 21b.
Alexander Caminada/Rex Features: 24c. Mark Clarke/SPL: 11tr. Stuart Clarke/Rex Features:
25b. Pablo Corral/Corbis: 30t. Deep Light/SPL:19t. Colin Edwards/Photofusion: 34t. Chris
Fairclough: 4, 9, 14, 36, 41, 45. Owen Franken/Corbis: 16b. A. Glauberman/SPL:18c. Paul
Hardy/Corbis: 17b. Hayley Madden/S.I.N/Corbis: 40c. Faye Norman/SPL: 22c. Claire Paxton
& Jacqui Farrow/SPL: 26c. Mark Peterson/Corbis: 29b, 31b. Harvey Pincis/SPL: 12c. James
Prince/SPL: 35c. Joel W. Rogers/Corbis: 28b. Saturn Stills/SPL: 37t. Chuck Savage/Corbis:
39c. Christopher Smith/Corbis: 23b. Roman Soumar/Corbis: 29t. Stapleton Collection,
UK/Bridgeman Art Library: 10b. Tom Stewart/Corbis: 38c. James A. Sugar/Corbis: 21c.
Swim Ink/Corbis: 11b. Charles Sykes/Rex Features: 32b. Tek Image/SPL: 13bl. Jonathan
Torgovnik/Corbis: 27t. Nik Wheeler/Corbis: 31t. Richard Young/Rex Features: 15c.

The Publisher would like to thank the Brunswick Club for Young People, Fulham, London
for their help with this book. Thanks to our models, including Elliott Scott, Stevie Waite
and Eva Webb.

A CIP catalogue record for this book is available from the British Library.

ISBN-10: 0 7496 5567 4
ISBN-13: 978 0 7496 5567 9

Printed in Malaysia

Franklin Watts is a division of Hachette Children's Books.

Contents

What is tobacco?

Tobacco is made from the dried leaves of the tobacco plant. The tobacco plant is a member of the same botanical family as potatoes and tomatoes. It is grown in more than 100 countries around the world, and processed into a variety of products including cigarettes, cigars, pipe tobacco, 'chew' tobacco and snuff powder. Of these, cigarettes are by far the most popular.

The world's 1.2 billion smokers smoke an estimated 20 billion cigarettes every single day.

Cigarettes

Cigarettes are made from dried tobacco, paper, a variety of additives and, in most cases, a filter. Hand-rolled cigarettes may not have a filter. When a cigarette is lit the tobacco breaks down into ash and smoke. The smoker inhales the smoke through the filter into the throat and lungs.

According to the tobacco industry, tobacco creates more employment per hectare of cultivated land than any other crop in the world.

It's your experience

'I don't see what all the fuss is about. My parents and my brother smoke but I don't mind. Everyone does it. I think there are far more important problems in the world.'

Sam, aged 12

Nicotine

Tobacco contains nicotine. Nicotine is a type of drug known as a 'stimulant' because it stimulates the central nervous system, increasing the heartbeat rate and raising blood pressure.

Nicotine is an addictive drug, which means that smokers find it difficult to be without it and may suffer withdrawal symptoms. It is also poisonous if taken in sufficient strength. Nevertheless, nicotine is a legal drug in every country in the world.

Additives

The tobacco in cigarettes contains a wide range of additives such as preservatives and flavourings. These are not listed as ingredients on cigarette packets but are generally designed to keep the tobacco fresh, to mask any unpleasant taste or smell and to increase the appeal to smokers.

In some countries over 600 additives are allowed to be added to cigarettes. Some people think that not enough is known about the effects of these additives on our health.

Oral tobacco

Not all tobacco users smoke cigarettes. In India and parts of Africa and Southeast Asia people chew the dried leaves ('areca') or a mixture of tobacco, leaves and spices ('betel quids'). The leaves are chewed to release the juices and the rest is spat out.

Oral tobacco avoids health problems associated with smoke, but users cannot avoid the dangers of nicotine addiction and the powerful cancer-causing compounds known as nitrosamines present in all tobacco. Research indicates that oral tobacco users are 50 times more likely to develop oral cancer. Despite this, the use of oral or 'spit' tobacco is on the increase among young males in the USA.

It's your decision

Are you concerned about the environment? Some anti-smoking campaigners think that people who decide to smoke should be more aware of the environmental consequences. They say that the production of tobacco involves the intensive use of pesticides and pollution from toxic chemical waste. In order to fuel the drying process it is also responsible for approximately one-eighth of the world's deforestation.

Do we know exactly what we are smoking?

The history of smoking

Historians believe that Native Americans began using tobacco for medicinal and ceremonial purposes over 2,000 years ago. However, tobacco was not introduced into Europe until Spanish and Portuguese explorers brought it back from the Americas at the end of the fifteenth century.

Snuff, cigars and cigarettes

At first tobacco was smoked in pipes, but by the end of the seventeenth century the sniffing of powdered tobacco, called 'snuff', was becoming increasingly widespread. Cigars became fashionable amongst the wealthy in the nineteenth century, and poor people soon learned to save the tobacco from discarded stubs in order to re-roll it between strips of paper. The cigarette had arrived.

The twentieth century

Cigarettes became increasingly popular as mechanised production methods and more efficient means of distribution made them cheaper and easier to buy. By the outbreak of the First World War in 1914, smoking had become a mass habit. Tobacco companies such as Philip Morris in the US, and British American Tobacco in the UK, expanded rapidly and began to sell their products in new markets overseas.

Snuff-taking was a social habit enjoyed by the wealthy in the eighteenth century.

During the Second World War (1939–45), US soldiers were issued with cigarettes as part of their rations. In the 1940s, about 65 per cent of men and 41 per cent of women in the UK were smokers.

Since the 1960s, smoking rates among adults in developed countries have generally declined. However, in many developing countries in the Far East and Africa, smoking is on the increase.

It's your experience

'When I was a girl my brother told me that smoking helped to keep colds away. We all smoked back then. I know it is bad for me but I've lasted this long and I am not going to give up now.'

Margaret, aged 94

"SEND SMOKES TO SAMMY!"

"FIFTY-FIFTY ON MY LAST SMOKE, BILL!"

Mail Your Contributions to

"OUR BOYS IN FRANCE TOBACCO FUND"

West 44th Street   Endorsed by War Department   New York City

A poster from 1918 asks Americans to support the war effort by sending cigarettes to the troops in the First World War.

Research into smoking

The ill-effects of smoking on the throat and lungs were noted from as early as the seventeenth century. However, many people insisted on the medicinal qualities of tobacco, and smoking was not publicly linked to cancer until 1951.

Researchers began to investigate the chemical content of cigarette smoke, but the tobacco industry disputed their findings and refused to accept that nicotine was addictive. Nevertheless some governments began to listen to the advice of anti-smoking campaigners. The first health warning appeared on cigarette packets in the USA in 1965, in the UK in 1971, and in Australia in 1972.

It's your opinion

◆ Why do you think that the tobacco companies were reluctant to accept that nicotine is addictive?
◆ What reasons can you think of to explain the rise in smoking in developing countries?

What happens when we smoke?

When we inhale – breathe in – a lighted cigarette, the burning tobacco reaches temperatures of up to 700 degrees Celsius at the tip. This causes a number of chemical reactions to take place, including the formation of gases such as carbon monoxide and of tiny droplets of sticky solids, known as tar.

Tobacco smoke contains around 4,000 chemical compounds. Many are present in tiny, insignificant amounts, but some are more toxic and are known to cause cancer.

In the lungs

When we draw tobacco smoke into our lungs it irritates the delicate lining of the air passages, which may make us cough or experience a burning sensation. The brown, treacly tar condenses and sticks to the walls of our bronchioles and alveoli. This interferes with the lungs' ability to fight infection and makes us more vulnerable to colds, flu, bronchitis and pneumonia. It also makes it more difficult for oxygen to pass from the lungs into the bloodstream. Some of the tar remains in our lungs but the rest is gradually absorbed through the lung walls.

It's your experience

'The first time I smoked was awful. I thought my throat was burning and I felt really sick. I got used to it pretty quickly though. And I liked the buzz it gave me. But now when I light up I don't feel anything at all.'

Jack, aged 18

In the bloodstream

Once the chemicals from tobacco smoke get into our bloodstream, they are transported rapidly around the body. Carbon monoxide reduces the amount of oxygen in the blood, because it binds with haemoglobin in red blood cells more easily than oxygen. This makes our heart and lungs work harder. It can also reduce our ability to think quickly.

In the brain

It takes between 8 and 15 seconds for nicotine to travel from our lungs to the brain, and this, for most of us, is the main purpose of smoking. Nicotine stimulates the receptors in the brain, which increases our heart rate and blood pressure and generates feelings of pleasure. This is the dizzy sensation or smoking 'high' which new smokers experience.

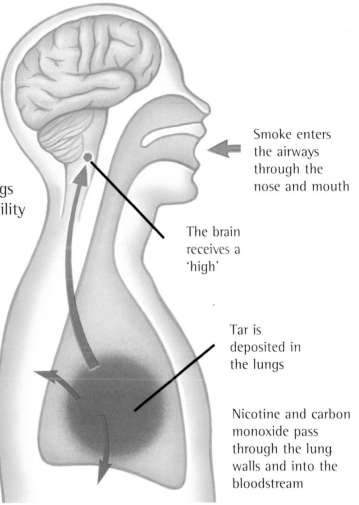

Smoke enters the airways through the nose and mouth

The brain receives a 'high'

Tar is deposited in the lungs

Nicotine and carbon monoxide pass through the lung walls and into the bloodstream

▲ Smoking affects your lungs, blood and brain.

▼ Special machines 'smoke' cigarettes to test their chemical content.

It's your decision

High tar, low tar or no tar?
Some of us choose to buy cigarettes labelled 'low in tar'. This usually means that they have a perforated filter that allows air to mix with cigarette smoke. However, anti-smoking campaigners argue that addicted smokers compensate for lower levels of nicotine by smoking more cigarettes or inhaling more deeply.

Why do people start smoking?

Most people start smoking between the ages of 11 and 15. In the USA and UK, over 80 per cent of adult smokers began in their teens.

Why so young?

There are many reasons why young people start smoking, ranging from curiosity, the influence of other smokers in the family, rebellion, pressure from friends to the belief that smoking is glamorous, or exciting. For some of us it is the desire to be part of a group, while for others it is about breaking away from the safety of childhood.

There is also a growing body of evidence to suggest that advertising is responsible for projecting an image of smoking that is particularly attractive to young people (see pages 28–29).

Family and friends

We are all influenced by what other people think and do. There is nothing wrong with this, but it can become a problem if we are under too much pressure to behave in a certain way. The tobacco industry argues that smoking among young people is a problem of society. It insists that most smokers take up the habit as a result of family or peer pressure.

Certainly, children are more likely to smoke if both of their parents smoke, and numerous studies have shown that most young smokers are influenced by their friends' and older siblings' smoking habits.

Older friends and siblings can influence smoking habits. ▼

It's your experience

'I go into town every Saturday with a group of friends from school. They all smoke, but at first I didn't want to. Then my friends started talking about going without me so I started smoking too. I know it's not good for me but I don't want to be left out.'

Emma, aged 14

It's your decision

Are you adventurous?
The tobacco company, Philip Morris, has suggested that the decision to start smoking is a symbolic act. 'I am no longer my mother's child, I'm tough, I am an adventurer, I'm not square... As the force from the psychological symbolism subsides, the pharmacological [drug] effect takes over to sustain the habit.'

Images like this suggest that smoking is glamorous and fun.

Influence of the media

Films, television, music and magazines are very good at creating an image or a lifestyle that we would like to have. When a film star or a famous model lights a cigarette it looks glamorous. A recent World Health Organisation survey has examined the Indian film industry and found that young people who watch their favourite actors smoke are three times more likely to do so themselves. The survey also found that these same young people are 16 times more likely to think positively about smoking.

Addiction

People start smoking for all sorts of reasons, but most continue to smoke for one reason only – they are addicted to nicotine. Addiction occurs when we take a drug that changes the way we feel and on which we become increasingly dependent, both in order to continue to experience its effects and to avoid the discomfort of its absence.

Rapid addiction
It is not only long-term smokers who are addicted to nicotine. Children who smoke as little as one cigarette a day can show signs of physical dependence after just four weeks.

The nicotine effect
The addictive effect of nicotine is linked to its capacity to trigger the release of dopamine – a chemical in the brain that is associated with feelings of pleasure. Once the drug wears off, we want another cigarette. For many this desire comes from an addiction that is both mental and physical.

Physical addiction
Physical addiction occurs when our bodies become used to having a certain amount of nicotine in the blood. Without further doses of nicotine we begin to experience discomfort in the form of withdrawal symptoms such as irritability, restlessness, anxiety and even depression.

In many developing countries, young people have little access to information about addiction.

It's your decision
Will cigarettes help you to concentrate? Many smokers believe that cigarettes help them to concentrate , but research suggests that all they are doing is temporarily suppressing the withdrawal symptoms caused by not smoking.

Mental addiction

Mental addiction occurs because nicotine is both stimulating and relaxing. Over time we learn to use these effects to cope with negative feelings and emotions such as boredom, or stress. We develop a psychological dependence.

Habit-forming

Smoking is often referred to as a 'habit', and this too is a form of mental addiction, as our brains learn to associate smoking with specific activities such as having a drink or watching TV. These habits can be very hard to break.

It's your experience

'I've been smoking since I was 15. My urge to smoke is triggered by all sorts of things like stress and tiredness, or eating or relaxing. Watching someone else light up makes me want a cigarette. Even talking about smoking creates a craving.'

Paul, aged 43

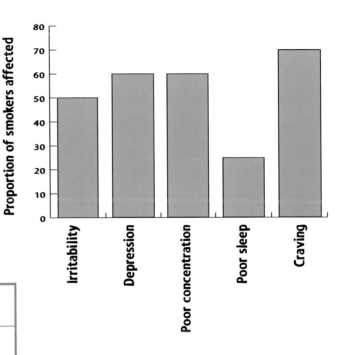

Symptoms of addiction to nicotine: proportion of smokers affected

Proportion of smokers affected

Symptom of addiction to nicotine

Difficulty in quitting

Nicotine is a powerfully addictive drug. Surveys show that at least 70 per cent of smokers want to stop smoking, yet only about three per cent succeed in quitting using willpower alone and few smokers believe that they could manage to go without a cigarette for a whole day. Some scientists argue that nicotine is as addictive as the illegal drugs heroin and cocaine.

Some people, particularly young women, don't want to quit because they believe that smoking helps to suppress their appetite.

Drinking alcohol and watching the television trigger the urge to smoke for many people.

Smoking and disease

We have all been told that smoking is bad for us. Nevertheless, most of us prefer to think that we can stop smoking before disease takes hold. According to the statistics, this is a mistake. About half of all regular smokers will eventually be killed by the habit.

Non-fatal diseases

Even if smoking does not prove fatal, smokers are more likely to suffer from an impaired immune system and a wide range of non-fatal illnesses such as impotence, psoriasis, hearing problems, coughs, chest pains and gum disease. They may also have bad breath, stained fingers and yellow teeth.

Cancer

Cigarette smoke contains at least 60 carcinogens, or cancer-causing compounds. These are absorbed through the mouth, throat and lungs, which is why cancers in these parts of our bodies are most commonly found in smokers. It is estimated that over 80 per cent of all deaths from lung cancer are due to smoking. However, the carcinogens also leak into our bloodstream and cause cancers in other organs including the bladder, kidneys, stomach and pancreas.

The lung specimen on the right is from a smoker, while the one on the left is from a non-smoker. The smoker's lung is darker, rougher and misshapen.

Heart disease and strokes

A smoker is two to three times more likely to have a heart attack than a non-smoker. This is because smoking affects the steady supply of blood to the heart.

Nicotine raises blood pressure by causing blood vessels to contract, forcing the heart to work harder, while carbon monoxide reduces the heart's effectiveness by lowering the amount of oxygen in the blood. Smoking also thickens the walls of our arteries and makes our blood clot, which may lead to a sudden blockage, resulting in a heart attack or a stroke.

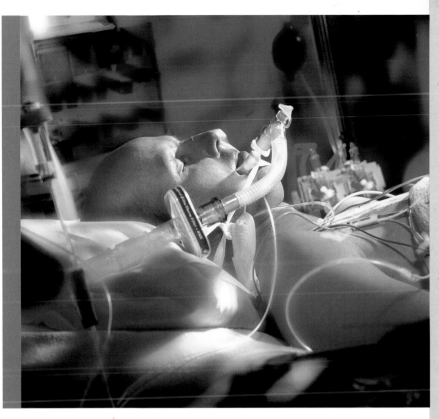

This man is breathing with the aid of a respirator after heart surgery. Smoking causes 25 per cent of heart disease deaths.

Divided opinion

Over the last decade, growing numbers of smokers who have contracted lung diseases have tried to sue the tobacco companies. The tobacco industry has argued that the impact of smoking on the health of a specific individual is too difficult to assess, and that anyway, health warnings have been printed on cigarette packets for over 40 years.

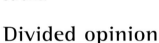

It's your opinion

Do you think that smokers' claims for compensation payments from tobacco companies are justified?

It's your decision

Do you want to start smoking now? The younger we are when we decide to smoke, the more dangerous it is. Someone who starts smoking aged 15 is three times more likely to die of cancer due to smoking than someone who starts in their mid-20s. This is partly because a younger person is likely to smoke for a greater number of years, but recent studies have also indicated that smoking in our teens can cause permanent genetic changes in the lungs which forever increase the risk of lung cancer.

Smoking and sport

Smoking affects our physical performance. The advice of all the major sporting bodies and organisations is that people who participate in sport should not smoke. In the long term, continued smoking damages our lungs and puts a strain on our hearts, making exercise increasingly difficult.

Can a smoker reach the peak of physical fitness?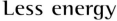

Less energy

When we exercise our muscles require more oxygen. Our lungs and heart need to work efficiently in order to supply this oxygen, and to remove the waste product carbon dioxide from the body.

Yet when we smoke the nicotine makes our arteries contract, while the carbon monoxide we inhale reduces the amount of oxygen our blood can absorb. Our muscles have less energy. We tire more quickly, and become more breathless than we would if we had not had a cigarette. Nevertheless, a smoker who exercises regularly is likely to be in better health than a smoker who never exercises at all.

Secret smokers

Very few sports people who are competing at the top level admit to smoking. Most do not smoke, but for some the addictive power of nicotine is so great that they continue to do so, despite the risk to their physical performance and their mental concentration. The pressure on them as role models means that they are too afraid of disappointing fans and attracting criticism to admit to their addiction.

Sponsorship

Most sporting events are funded by sponsors in exchange for the opportunity to promote their own products and services. Tobacco companies like to sponsor sport because it is watched by millions on TV and because it presents an image of adventure and success that corresponds with the image of many cigarette brands.

The European Union is banning all tobacco-related sponsorship of sport in its member countries because it believes that it encourages young smokers to take up the habit. However, some people argue that this means that events like Formula 1 will simply re-locate to countries where there are fewer restrictions and greater numbers of potential smokers, such as China.

It's your experience

'I have never had a problem with our young players smoking. They are all aware of the health risks and none of them want to jeopardise their place on the team.'

Head coach of the academy at Manchester United Football Club

A sports fan celebrates with a cigar. Tobacco is often given away free at sports events.

It's your opinion

Sponsorship deals mean more money for sport. Do you think that tobacco companies should be allowed to sponsor events such as Formula 1 and snooker?

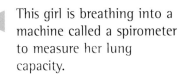

This girl is breathing into a machine called a spirometer to measure her lung capacity.

Passive smoking

When a cigarette is lit, smoke from the burning tip combines with the smoker's exhaled smoke to form what is known as environmental tobacco smoke, or ETS. Breathing in other people's ETS is called 'passive smoking'. Anti-smoking groups have been concerned about the effects of passive smoking for over 30 years.

Is it harmful?

Many studies have been published to suggest that passive smokers are exposed to some of the risks faced by smokers themselves, including lung cancer and heart disease. However, the evidence has been hotly disputed and the tobacco companies continue to maintain that while passive smoking may be unpleasant, it has not been proved to damage our health.

Many children are exposed to ETS in their homes. ▼

Passive smoking and children

According to the World Health Organisation, almost half the world's children are exposed to other people's tobacco smoke. For young children, this smoke is mainly from parents and other family members in the home. This raises serious health issues because many studies have found a link between passive smoking in children and asthma, bronchitis, pneumonia and middle-ear infections.

Pregnancy

Unborn children are also affected by passive smoking. When a pregnant woman smokes, the chemicals in her blood pass into the bloodstream of the foetus. This is believed to contribute to low birth weight and cot death (SIDS) in young babies.

▼ Smoking while pregnant can lead to the baby being smaller than average and can reduce its chances of survival.

It's your experience

I suffer from asthma. My doctor says that asthma is caused by all sorts of things, but I know that if I go into a smoky room or sit next to someone who is smoking, I am much more likely to have an asthma attack.

Jamal, aged 13

Public places

Bans on smoking in public places are becoming increasingly widespread, particularly in the developed countries. In New York, USA, smoking is now banned in all restaurants with more than 35 seats and in almost all buildings used by the public. In the UK there are now non-smoking areas on some beaches.

However, it is difficult to measure the health benefits of such bans. They are popular with non-smokers but the owners of restaurants and bars often worry that a smoking ban may lead to a fall in the number of customers. Even some non-smokers say that people should be allowed the right to smoke in bars.

It's your decision

Pro-smoking campaigners argue that to ban smoking in public places is to deny smokers their right to personal freedom. Anti-smoking campaigners argue that smoking in public places denies non-smokers their right to a healthy environment. Whose rights matter most?

▲ Patrons of a New York bar have to smoke outside.

The law

Many countries have laws to protect children from the dangers of smoking and measures to increase public awareness about tobacco and its effects. The USA and the European Union have passed laws concerning clearer labelling of the nicotine and tar content of a packet of cigarettes, more explicit health warnings and less advertising. However, in some parts of the world cigarettes are not so heavily regulated.

Here a newsagent refuses to sell a child cigarettes, but some retailers ignore the law.

The law and young people

Many laws about smoking are intended to prevent young people from taking up the habit. In the UK, it is illegal for anyone to sell cigarettes to a person who appears to be under 16. A retailer can be fined up to £1,000 if caught. In Australia the legal age is 18 and fines for retailers can be much higher. In Wisconsin, USA it is illegal for under-18s to possess or use tobacco, and young people are fined themselves if they are caught.

Taxes

Most countries tax the sale of tobacco, which means that an additional charge must be included in the price of every packet of cigarettes. In some countries this amounts to as much as 80 per cent of the total cost of a pack of cigarettes.

This has two purposes: to raise revenue for the government, and to reduce smoking. The World Bank concludes that when the price of cigarettes is increased, consumption falls.

Smuggling

Higher taxes mean that more people will try to avoid paying them. Smugglers illegally import cigarettes on which no tax is paid, and sell them at hugely discounted prices.

Smuggled cigarettes are not only a problem for the police and customs agencies. The fact that they are much cheaper means that more young people want to smoke them.

It's your opinion

In New York in 2002 a judge ordered a woman not to smoke in her home or in her car because of the potential harm to her healthy son, who objected to tobacco smoke. Do you think this kind of legal intervention is acceptable, or justified?

It's your decision

The British government says, 'We are not going to ban smoking. We accept that smokers have a right to choose to smoke, but we also have a responsibility to reduce smoking and save lives.' The government tries to curb smoking by making it more and more expensive. Yet many people continue to smoke despite the cost.

This problem is made worse by the Internet. Cigarettes on which no tax has been paid can be bought online by young people who do not have to prove their age. Legislation in some countries is attempting to deal with this issue, but smuggling and tax evasion are likely to continue.

Customs officials seize smuggled cigarettes and alcohol.

The costs of smoking

As well as being expensive for individuals, smoking costs society as a whole, mainly through medical costs for smoking-related illness, the costs of house and forest fires and business costs for time off work. The actual cost is difficult to assess however because this must be balanced by income from taxation, donations by tobacco companies and jobs and wealth created by the tobacco industry.

A doctor shows a young woman a leaflet on quitting smoking. Society pays for the prevention of smoking-related disease, as well as its treatment.

It's your experience

'I don't know how much money I've spent on cigarettes over the last three years. I don't think I want to know.'

Megan, aged 17

Health costs and taxes

In the USA is has been estimated that a packet of cigarettes has a social cost of $3.45 in treating smoking-related diseases. In the UK the National Health Service spends £1.7 billion each year on treating the effects of smoking. These costs are often compared with the amount of tax raised by the government from the sale of cigarettes, which in the UK amounts to over £9 billion.

Anti-smoking campaigners point out that taxes must be raised from somewhere, and research shows that putting up the cost of cigarettes encourages smokers to quit. However, more non-smokers means less tax for the government, and pro-smoking organisations argue that because smokers die younger, they actually cost the state less in medical expenses and social security payments.

Division of money spent on drug-related health problems in Australia, 2003

22% alcohol

17% illegal drugs

61% smoking

A young street boy smoking in India.

Industry and employment

Smoking is expensive for employers. Smoking-related illness means time off work and smokers and their employers pay higher insurance costs. A Canadian study has found that smoking breaks while at work cost employers over $2,000 per smoker per year.

The tobacco industry counters that it employs over 100 million people worldwide, but the World Bank has concluded that a global fall in tobacco consumption would mean that 'more jobs are likely to be created than lost'. The leisure and tourism industries in particular would benefit from more healthy, wealthy non-smokers.

Smoking and poverty

Higher taxes on cigarettes may deter some of us from smoking, but the nature of addiction means that many people will continue to smoke. In developing countries the cost of smoking can have a direct impact on malnutrition. A study in Bangladesh has shown that poorer people who smoke spend less on the family's food in order to pay for their habit.

It's your decision

Will smoking affect your job prospects? If a non-smoker and a smoker both apply for the same job and the employer is aware that smokers generally take more time off work, he or she is more likely to choose the non-smoker.

Advertising

Tobacco companies advertise their products in many different ways. When permitted, they place advertisements in magazines, on television, on roadside billboards and in shop windows. They may sponsor events, offer free gifts and even pay to have their products smoked by celebrities. They also place brand 'reminders' such as stickers at the point of sale in convenience stores and supermarkets.

The power of advertising

The tobacco companies have entered into agreements which regulate their advertising. Nevertheless, most of us are exposed to some form of tobacco advertising on a regular basis. The Campaign for Tobacco-Free Kids says that young people are three times more sensitive to tobacco advertising than adults and that one third of underage experimentation with smoking is due to tobacco company advertising.

Brand-selling

The tobacco industry argues that peer pressure remains the biggest influence on first-time smokers and advertising only affects the brand they choose.

In the USA, over 80 per cent of young smokers prefer the three most heavily advertised brands, compared to less than half of adult smokers. This is because new young smokers are more influenced by image than by other factors such as price, or taste.

Anti-smoking campaigners believe that 'Joe Camel' encouraged under-age smoking.

"हम रेड एण्ड व्हाईट पीने वालों की बात ही कुछ और है!"

RED &
WHITE
FILTER

It's your opinion

Think about some of the tobacco advertising you have come across recently. What do you remember about it? What message was it trying to get across? Did it make an impact on you?

◀ Tobacco advertising on a wall in India.

Changing times

Some forms of tobacco advertising such as billboards and sponsorship deals, are becoming illegal, and TV advertising is not allowed in many countries, yet the tobacco industry knows it has to attract new smokers if it is to survive. When billboard advertisements were banned in the USA, tobacco promotions in convenience stores significantly increased. Tobacco companies can still place their cigarettes in films in most countries, and trade unrelated goods such as clothes under cigarette brand names to advertise their products.

New restrictions on tobacco advertising are being introduced all the time, but loopholes remain and in many of the biggest markets in Southeast Asia and Africa, there are very few restrictions at all.

It's your decision

Does advertising persuade you?
The tobacco companies say that they do not aim their advertising at young non-smokers. Anti-smoking campaigners disagree. They say that sophisticated adult-targetted advertising makes cigarettes even more appealing to children.

▲ Tobacco advertising on the door of a convenience store.

The power of tobacco companies

Cigarettes mean big business for the handful of companies that dominate the global tobacco market. Their profits are huge and their business is multinational; brands like Marlboro are marketed worldwide.

In Argentina this man's sunhat becomes a marketing tool.

Misuse of power?

In the past, the tobacco industry has been accused of exploiting poor farmers, unfairly influencing government decisions about smoking policy, and covering up research about the damaging effects of cigarettes. However, in the light of the overwhelming evidence about the dangers of smoking, the tobacco companies are now redefining themselves as socially responsible employers, funding youth smoking prevention programmes and establishing voluntary codes of conduct. British American Tobacco says 'We believe in adding value to the communities in which we operate.'

Nevertheless, anti-smoking campaigners insist that the industry continues to misuse its power. Many tobacco companies have now diversified into other products, including food manufacture and finance. This means that many people are investing in tobacco companies without realising it.

Threats to the industry

In high-income countries, smoking among adults is generally declining. This is mainly due to better information about health issues, new restrictions on advertising and high levels of tax. Some tobacco companies are having to pay out huge sums in compensation payments to smokers.

Fighting back

However, the tobacco industry's arguments for commercial freedom of speech continue to influence many international trading agreements, and the big tobacco companies are expanding into new markets in lower-income countries with fewer restrictions and less health awareness.

New recruits

In the developing world, approximately 48 per cent of men and 7 per cent of women currently smoke. Given the huge populations of countries like China and India, a small increase in smoking among women would greatly increase the size of the world tobacco market.

The big tobacco companies are already tapping into this potential by promoting brands such as Virginia Slims as modern, sophisticated and 'western'. The result is a new demand, especially among women and young people. By the mid 2020s it is predicted that about 85 per cent of the world's smokers will live in developing countries which are least able to fight an epidemic of addiction and disease.

◀ The World Health Organisation has estimated that the number of women who smoke will almost triple over the next generation, to more than 500 million.

It's your opinion

▶ The USA has a Cigarette Advertising and Promotion Code to regulate the activities of the tobacco industry. It is not applied to the activities of American tobacco companies in other countries because it says that it would be wrong to impose American values on other societies. Anti-smoking campaigners think that this is hypocritical. What do you think?

In 2000 Nottingham University received £3.8 million from British American Tobacco to fund an International Centre for Corporate Social Responsibility. Some teachers and professors decided to resign in protest. Do you think they had a point?

▲ Cigarette production at the R.J. Reynolds plant in North Carolina, USA.

Anti-smoking campaigns

Anti-smoking campaigns are usually initiated by health workers, government policymakers, or pressure groups such as Action on Smoking and Health (ASH). Generally they have one or more of three aims: to prevent young people from smoking in the first place; to persuade existing smokers to quit; and to protect people from the dangers of passive smoking.

Which ones work?

Different campaigns work best for different groups of people. Information 'shocks' or widely publicised official reports on the dangers of smoking tend to have the greatest impact where general awareness of the health risks is low. As knowledge increases, new information shocks become less effective, although they do continue to contribute to a general drop in smoking.

School programmes

School anti-smoking programmes are widespread, yet although many young people who smoke remember health education lessons, they choose to ignore them. Researchers say this is because young people tend to be less influenced by information about the long-term effects of smoking and more concerned with rebellion against adult advice.

Some recent campaigns have focused on less life-threatening problems, such as yellow teeth, bad breath and bad skin, in order to get their message across. The Australian government has sponsored a Smoke Free Fashion initiative to challenge the idea that smoking is fashionable and to avoid images that might encourage young people to smoke.

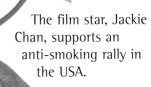

The film star, Jackie Chan, supports an anti-smoking rally in the USA.

Graphic health warnings

Since the 1960s a growing number of governments have required cigarette manufacturers to print health warnings on their products. These vary from small printed messages to graphic colour pictures of lung tumours, diseased hearts and rotting teeth. In Canada, such images have covered the top half of both sides of cigarette packets since 2001 and 44 per cent of smokers say that this has increased their motivation to quit.

Such campaigns are likely to be less effective in poorer countries where cigarettes are often sold singly, instead of in packs.

It's your experience

'I know that millions of people die every year from smoking, but I've never taken much notice of the statistics. I stopped when my boyfriend said my breath smelled bad.'

Janine, aged 16

Smoking kills

Smoking harms your baby

Smoking is highly addictive, don't start

Smoking seriously harms you and others around you

Smokers die younger

Health warnings on cigarette packets are becoming less easy to ignore.

WARNING
CIGARETTES
CAUSE MOUTH
DISEASES

Cigarette smoke causes oral cancer, gum diseases and tooth loss.

Health Canada

Player's

25 FILTER

It's your opinion

What type of anti-smoking campaign is likely to influence you most, and why?

California: a case study

In 1988, California significantly raised tobacco taxes and spent 20 per cent of the revenue on an aggressive public education campaign. Over the next decade it banned smoking in public places, such as offices and restaurants. The result was a 16 per cent fall in California's lung cancer rate, compared with a drop of 2.7 per cent in the rest of the USA.

Smoking other drugs

Drugs are chemical substances that cause changes in the mind or the body. Many drugs are used legally for medicinal purposes. Some drugs such as tobacco, alcohol and caffeine are also legal but are used for recreational purposes. Other 'recreational' drugs such as cannabis, heroin, ecstasy and cocaine are illegal because they are considered to be more dangerous, more addictive, or simply less acceptable to society as a whole. However, tobacco has been shown to be a far bigger killer than all other drugs put together.

Cannabis smokers tend to inhale more deeply than smokers of conventional cigarettes.

Cannabis

Cannabis is made from the dried leaves of the cannabis plant. Like tobacco, it is usually smoked. It induces feelings of relaxation and euphoria, and its physical effects include increased pulse rate, mild pain reduction and dizziness. It is not physically addictive. Evidence suggests that it has some medical benefits including the relief of symptoms of multiple sclerosis, and there is a vigorous debate in many countries about whether it should in fact be made legal. Some people argue that it should remain illegal because cannabis use might lead to the misuse of more dangerous drugs. They also say that not enough is known about the effects of cannabis – it may cause cancer in the same way as tobacco.

However, perhaps the biggest health concern is that cannabis is usually mixed with tobacco and smoked in hand-rolled cigarettes or 'joints' without a filter. Cannabis smokers also tend to inhale particularly deeply. Researchers say that smoking three cannabis cigarettes a day may be as dangerous as smoking 20 conventional cigarettes.

Crack cocaine

Crack is a smokeable form of cocaine, which is extracted from the coca plant. When heated in a pipe, crack vaporises and is easily inhaled. As with many drugs it is highly addictive, and users can die from an overdose. Although crack does not contain the same substances found in tobacco, the smoke can seriously harm the lungs and cause chest pains. Crack is believed to be more rapidly addictive than other forms of cocaine because smoking it allows extremely high doses of the drug to reach the brain more quickly.

A man smokes crack cocaine with the aid of a small blowtorch.

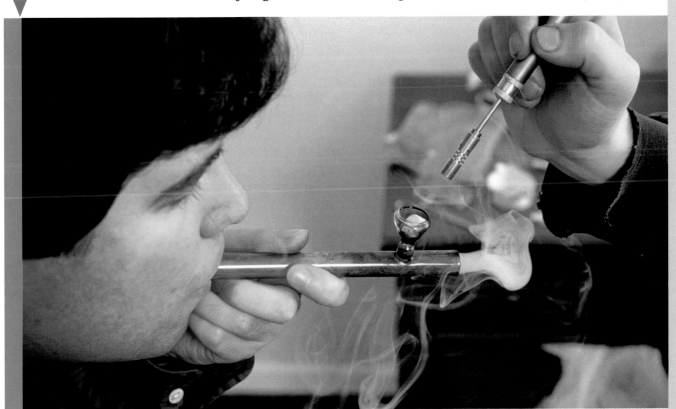

It's your experience

'No one I know thinks cannabis is dangerous. Some people are scared of drugs like heroin and crack, but cannabis is just like a cigarette. Most of our parents smoked it when they were younger, didn't they?'

Michael, aged 15

It's your decision

What do statistics prove?
Statistics show that 63 per cent of smokers have used illegal drugs, while only 1 per cent of non-smokers have used them. Some people argue that this proves that smoking leads to drug misuse. However, we can choose not to use illegal drugs, just as we can choose not to use tobacco products.

Giving up

Giving up smoking is not easy. In the UK, nearly a half of smokers aged 11 to 15 want to quit, yet almost two-thirds have failed at the first attempt. In the USA nearly 60 per cent of teenage smokers try and fail to quit each year. This is because they have become addicted to nicotine.

Giving up takes mental commitment and determination to confront the physical symptoms of nicotine withdrawal. Many quitters try several times before they stop smoking for good.

Motivation and support

No one else can make us give up smoking. Sometimes, being told that we ought to give up is not helpful because it can create feelings of failure and hopelessness. We have to want to do it for ourselves. Nevertheless, once someone decides they want to quit, it is vital that they get as much support from family and friends as possible. This is particularly important in beating the mental addiction. If other people know what triggers our desire for a cigarette, they may be able to help us avoid those situations.

Some people prefer to go to a support group where they can share their experiences with people who understand what they are going through. Others try hypnosis or acupuncture – although there is no evidence to prove whether these treatments genuinely help or not.

Having the support of someone who understands can boost our confidence and motivation to quit.

It's your experience

I always smoked my first cigarette of the day on the way to school. I couldn't give it up, but then I started cycling instead of walking. It's difficult to smoke on a bike.

Jon, aged 16

Nicotine patches release a controlled dose of nicotine into the body. ▶

Physical aids

Many smokers find it difficult to quit using willpower alone. A number of products have been shown to increase success rates for quitters, but they can be expensive and are not available to everyone.

Nicotine replacement therapy, or NRT is the most widely used aid. A range of patches, gums and sprays deliver a low dose of nicotine without delivering the other harmful elements of tobacco smoke. The idea is that the dose of nicotine is gradually reduced over a number of weeks until the user is free from dependence on nicotine altogether.

Buproprion is an anti-depressant drug available on prescription that attaches itself to the same receptors in the brain as nicotine. It prevents the user from going into nicotine withdrawal, and lessens the urge to smoke. However, buproprion may, on rare occasions, cause seizures.

Exercise

Some people find exercise helpful because it releases feel-good chemicals into the brain that may disguise some of the effects of nicotine withdrawal.

It's your decision

Some people decide to smoke fewer cigarettes rather than quit smoking altogether. Smoking two cigarettes a day is better for us than 20 cigarettes, but doctors point out that cutting down doesn't help us to give up – it merely reinforces the cycle of craving.

The good news!

Thousands of people do manage to stop smoking every day. If we give up smoking we can undo much of the damage to our health.

Health benefits

After only two days there is no nicotine left in the body. After one year the risk of a heart attack falls to about half that of a smoker. Other benefits include younger-looking skin, whiter teeth, fresher breath and more energy for sport.

◄ Giving up smoking improves our energy levels by increasing the amount of oxygen we can absorb.

It's your experience

'I thought it would be easy to give up, but on the third day I got really bored and had a cigarette. The next time I tried I had an argument with my dad, and gave in again. This time I'm going to do it. I know what to expect, and I don't want to be trying to stop all my life.'

Carla, aged 17

Time since quitting	Health benefits
20 minutes	Blood pressure and pulse rate return to normal.
8 hours	Oxygen levels return to normal.
24 hours	There is no carbon monoxide left in the body.
48 hours	There is no nicotine left in the body.
72 hours	Breathing becomes easier and energy levels increase.
One year	Risk of heart attack falls to half that of a smoker.

Help yourself
Most quitters find it useful to think carefully about ways in which cravings and difficult moments can be tackled, and overcome. A plan of action might include some of the following:

QUITTING HELP LIST

• If you have tried to stop in the past, think about what did and did not help.

• Identify those moments when you most want a cigarette, and think about how you might deal with them. Is your first cigarette of the day the one you crave the most? Would a small change to your morning routine be helpful?

• Which day of the week is best for you to stop: a weekday, or a weekend?

• Tell your friends that you are planning to quit, so that they can offer support. If they are unlikely to be supportive, tell them you are not smoking because of a sore throat.

• Some people eat more when they give up, and put on some extra weight. Decide what to about this in advance. You might choose to drink more water or chew sugar-free gum.

• Have a list of support groups and quitline phone numbers to hand, ready for those difficult moments.

It's your opinion
Do you think it is better to tell everyone when you are planning to give up, or does this just make you feel worse if you fail?

▲ What would you rather spend your money on?

Think of the money
Smoking costs a fortune. One of the best things about quitting is to work out how much money you will save each month, and what it can be spent on. Plan on treating yourself!

Making a choice

Cigarettes are bad for our health. Yet for most of us, choosing whether to smoke or not is about far more than understanding addiction and the damage tobacco can do to our bodies. It is about fitting in, growing up, building an identity and finding self-confidence. We all need to be aware of which issues are likely to influence our decision the most.

We don't need to smoke if we want to have a good time.

It's your decision

Can you say no?

No one can tell you what to do. However, if you are worried about smoking then practise saying no and give your reasons to a friend, or even to the mirror. The more we say no to cigarettes, the more confident we become in ourselves as non-smokers.

Self-image

Most of us, at some point in our lives, have a poor self-image. This might be to do with how attractive we feel, or how many friends we have. The tobacco companies are very good at promoting their products as cool, glamorous and sophisticated. Sometimes we hope that, by smoking, we can transform into more desirable, interesting people. However, there are plenty of successful non-smoking role models out there.

Peer pressure

Pressure from people around us to behave in a particular way can be very hard to resist. If our friends smoke, it is difficult not to join in. Everyone needs to be accepted, and rejection is particularly stressful for young people who are moving away from their parents and redefining their place in the world.

If peer pressure is a problem it might be better to seek out different friends. If this is difficult you could even make up a reason for not smoking, such as asthma.

Dealing with problems

Some people use smoking as a way to deal with boredom, or stress, or loneliness. For these people, the psychological prop of smoking can be particularly difficult to overcome.

It is worth remembering that smoking does not actually remove our problems. At best it may distract us for a minute, but it can add to feelings of stress or failure when addiction takes hold and we lose the ability to control our smoking habit.

It's your opinion

According to the Tobacco Manufacturers Association, 'Smoking is an adult pursuit and should remain a matter for informed and adult choice.' Others argue that someone who is addicted to nicotine is no longer capable of exercising free choice about smoking. What do you think?

Many young smokers say they would prefer not to smoke.

It's your health!

If you are at an age where you are legally allowed to smoke it is up to you to decide whether to smoke or not. It is an adult decision, based on whether you think the benefit to you of smoking is worth the risk to your health.

Have you made your choice?

Glossary

Acupuncture inserting needles into the skin to stimulate the body to heal itself

Addictive drug a drug that the body and mind can become dependent on

Additives substances such as preservatives and flavourings that are added to tobacco

Asthma a respiratory disease

Bronchitis inflammation of the airways

Buproprion an anti-depressant drug that lessens the urge to smoke

Cannabis the dried leaves of the cannabis plant

Carbon monoxide a poisonous gas present in tobacco smoke

Carcinogen cancer-causing compound

Crack a smokeable form of the illegal drug cocaine

Dopamine a chemical in the brain associated with feelings of pleasure

Emphysema a lung disease

Environmental tobacco smoke (ETS) a mix of exhaled tobacco smoke and the smoke from the burning tip of a cigarette

Hypnosis a therapy in which the subconscious mind is guided towards a desired outcome

Joint a hand-rolled cigarette made with cannabis

Low tar cigarettes with holes in the filter to allow air to mix with the smoke

Nicotine the addictive drug present in all tobacco products

Nicotine replacement therapy (NRT) patches, gums or sprays that deliver a controlled dose of nicotine without the harmful effects of smoke

Nitrosamines powerful cancer-causing compounds present in all tobacco

Oral tobacco any kind of tobacco which is chewed in the mouth

Passive smoking breathing in smoke from other people's cigarettes

Snuff powdered tobacco

Stimulant any drug which stimulates the central nervous system

Tar a harmful brown sticky substance found in cigarette smoke

Withdrawal symptoms feelings of anxiety, sleeplessness or irritability experienced by people who are addicted to nicotine

Further Information

QUIT
A UK charity that helps people give up smoking.

Quit, Ground Floor, 211 Old Street, London EC1V 9NR
www.quit.org.uk
Quit helpline: 0800 00 22 00
Asian quitline: 0800 00 22 88
Or email for sameday advice to stopsmoking@quit.org.uk

NHS Smoking Helpline
Freephone 0800 169 0 169

Action on Smoking and Health (ASH)
An anti-smoking organisation with information on current issues and legislation concerning passive smoking, smoking bans and smoking-related diseases.

102 Clifton St, London EC2A 4HW
www.ash.org.uk
Tel: 020 7739 5902

FOREST (Freedom Organisation for the Right to Enjoy Smoking Tobacco)
An organisation that defends the interests of smokers and promotes freedom of choice.

13 Palace St, London SW1E 5HX
www.forestonline.org

Cancer Research UK
PO Box 123, Lincoln's Inn Fields,
London
WC2A 3PX
Tel: 020 7242 0200
www.cancerresearchuk.org

Health Education Authority
Trevelyan House,
30 Great Peter Street,
London
SW1 2HW
www.hea.org.uk

AUSTRALIA
ASH (Australia)
153 Dowling Street,
Woolloomooloo 2011
www.ashaust.org.au

Quit Now
The Australian National Tobacco Campaign offers information on smoking and health and tips to stop smoking.

www.quitnow.info.au
Quitline number: 131 848

Australian Department of Health and Ageing
GPO Box 9848, Canberra
ACT 2601
Tel: 02 6289 1555
www.health.gov.au

The Cancer Council Australia
GPO Box 4708, Sydney NSW 2001
Tel: 02 9036 3100
www.cancer.org.au

The Australian Council on Smoking and Health (ACOSH)
Dedicated to raising awareness about smoking and health issues.

ACOSH,
Level 1,
46 Ventnor Avenue,
West Perth,
Western Australia 6005
www.acosh.org

Note to parents and teachers: Every effort has been made by the Publishers to ensure that these websites are suitable for children, that they are of the highest educational value, and that they contain no inappropriate or offensive material. However, because of the nature of the Internet, it is impossible to guarantee that the contents of these sites will not be altered. We strongly advise that Internet access is supervised by a responsible adult.

Index